FEB 1 1 2009

P9-CED-379

3 9077 06437 8311

DWAYNE "THE ROCK" JOHNSON

Marylou Morano Kjelle

P.O. Box 196
Hockessin, Delaware 19707
Visit us on the web: www.mitchelllane.com
Comments? email us: mitchelllane@mitchelllane.com

Mitchell Lane PUBLISHERS

Copyright © 2009 by Mitchell Lane Publishers. All rights reserved. No part of this book may be reproduced without written permission from the publisher. Printed and bound in the United States of America.

Printing   1   2   3   4   5   6   7   8   9

A Robbie Reader
Contemporary Biography

Albert Pujols	Alex Rodriguez	Aly and AJ
Amanda Bynes	Ashley Tisdale	Brittany Murphy
Charles Schulz	Dakota Fanning	Dale Earnhardt Jr.
Donovan McNabb	Drake Bell & Josh Peck	Dr. Seuss
Dwayne "The Rock" Johnson	Dylan & Cole Sprouse	Eli Manning
Hilary Duff	Jamie Lynn Spears	Jessie McCartney
Johnny Gruelle	The Jonas Brothers	Jordin Sparks
LeBron James	Mia Hamm	Miley Cyrus
Miranda Cosgrove	Raven Symone	Shaquille O'Neal
The Story of Harley-Davidson	Syd Hoff	Tiki Barber
Tom Brady	Tony Hawk	

Library of Congress Cataloging-in-Publication Data
Kjelle, Marylou Morano.
  Dwayne "the Rock" Johnson / by Marylou Morano Kjelle.
     p. cm. — (A Robbie reader)
  Includes bibliographical references and index.
  ISBN 978-1-58415-722-9 (library bound)
1. Rock (Wrestler) — Juvenile literature. 2. Wrestlers — United States — Biography — Juvenile literature. 3. Actors — United States — Biography — Juvenile literature. I. Title.
  GV1196.R63K54 2009
  796.812092 — dc22
  [B]

2008008067

ABOUT THE AUTHOR: Marylou Morano Kjelle has written dozens of books for young readers of all ages, many of them for Mitchell Lane Publishers. She teaches Writing at her alma mater, Rutgers University, and at other colleges in New Jersey. She also works as a reporter for several New Jersey newspapers, writing mostly about arts and entertainment. When she is not writing or teaching, Marylou reads, cooks, and watches movies.

AUTHOR'S NOTE: World Wrestling Federation (WWF) is now called World Wrestling Entertainment (WWE). In order to avoid going back and forth, I have consistently used WWF.

PUBLISHER'S NOTE: The following story has been thoroughly researched and to the best of our knowledge represents a true story. While every possible effort has been made to ensure accuracy, neither the publisher nor the author will assume liability for damages caused by inaccuracies in the data, and makes no warranty on the accuracy of the information contained herein. This story has not been authorized or endorsed by Dwayne Johnson.

PLB

TABLE OF CONTENTS

Words in **bold** type can be found in the glossary.

Dwayne played Mathayus in both *The Scorpion King* and *The Mummy Returns*. As a champion pro wrestler, Dwayne was already a larger-than-life character, so acting came easily to him.

The Rock Plays a King

When Dwayne Johnson walked onto the set of the movie *The Scorpion King*, he knew his life was about to change.

Dwayne had done many things in his life. He had played defensive tackle for his high school and college football teams. He had fought as a pro wrestler for the World Wrestling Federation (WWF) and been named a champion. He had written an **autobiography** (aw-toh-by-AH-gruh-fee), called *The Rock Says . . .* , which had become a bestselling book.

Dwayne had also worked as an actor. He had appeared in movies, on wrestling videos, and on television shows. But he had never had

The Rock and Michael Clarke Duncan at the premiere of *The Scorpion King* at the Universal Amphitheatre in Los Angeles, California. In the movie, Michael Duncan plays the tribal leader, Balthazar, who helps the Scorpion King defeat the evil king, Memnon.

a leading role in a movie. The actor who has the leading role is the movie's star. He plays the movie's most important character.

Dwayne's first leading role was in *The Scorpion King*. In this movie, he plays Mathayus, the last fighter left in a family of **ancient** warriors. Dwayne also played Mathayus in an earlier movie called *The Mummy Returns*.

There are many battles and other action scenes for Mathayus in both *The Mummy Returns* and *The Scorpion King.* This is exactly the type of character that Dwayne likes to play.

"The role was . . . made for me," said Dwayne. As Mathayus, he was able to be the tough guy his wrestling fans knew and loved. The role brought him new fans as well. People who did not follow wrestling started to notice that Dwayne had what it takes to be in the movies. Almost overnight, Dwayne went from wrestling star to movie star.

Dwayne was paid over $5 million for his role as Mathayus in *The Scorpion King.* His salary made history. It was the largest amount of money a male actor had ever earned for his first leading role.

Since filming *The Scorpion King* in 2002, Dwayne has gone on to make more movies. He enjoys playing different roles. He has played good guys and bad guys. But whether his characters are mean or nice, Dwayne loves being an entertainer.

Where in the World

Samoa
Islands

Fiji

South
Pacific
Ocean

Dwayne's mother, Ata, is from Samoa, a group of islands in the South
Pacific. Peter Maivia, Dwayne's grandfather, was a Samoan High Chief.

The Family Business

Dwayne Douglass Johnson was born on May 2, 1972, in Hayward, California. He is the only child of Rocky and Ata Johnson. Rocky is an African Canadian. Ata is from Samoa, a country of islands that lies near Australia in the South Pacific Ocean.

Dwayne knows the combination of his African and Samoan heritages has made him what he is today. "I'm very proud of what I am. That will never change," he told a reporter in 2002.

Peter Maivia

9

Wrestling is in Dwayne's blood. Rocky worked as a professional wrestler from the 1960s to the 1980s. Dwayne's grandfather, Peter Maivia, a Samoan High Chief, was a legendary heavyweight who won many wrestling awards. Many of Dwayne's Samoan uncles and cousins are also wrestling champions.

Eddie Fatu is another wrestler in Dwayne's family. Eddie is known as Umaga, the Samoan Bulldozer.

Dwayne's father, Rocky Johnson, started wrestling in the 1960s. Twenty years later, he became the first African American to win the World Wrestling Federation Intercontinental title. In addition to wrestling, Rocky is a swimmer, boxer, and gymnast.

Professional wrestlers work in many places. They often live away from their families for long periods of time. That wasn't the case with the Johnson family. Dwayne and Ata traveled with Rocky wherever his work took him. Before he started school, Dwayne had lived in five states and in the country of New Zealand.

At the wrestling matches, Dwayne and Ata would sit close to the ring. Dwayne watched every move that Rocky made. He loved to watch the wrestling moves, and the way wrestling tested a wrestler's ability. He loved the way the fans cheered the players they liked and booed the ones they did not. "I was fascinated by the business," said Dwayne. "I loved everything about it."

After the matches, when he was back home, Dwayne pretended to be his father. He wore Rocky's championship belts around his chest, and he practiced wrestling moves like dropkicks and headlocks.

When he was eight years old, Dwayne told Rocky that he wanted to be a wrestler. Even at such a young age, Dwayne knew that professional wrestling is an act. When two wrestlers enter a ring, they know who will win and who will lose a match. All the moves in a wrestling ring are staged, like a performance. Each wrestler knows what to expect from his opponent. Maybe one player will get thrown against the ropes or get caught in a headlock.

Rocky Johnson (left) and professional wrestler Tony Atlas were the first black wrestlers to win the WWF Tag Team Championship. They defeated a team of Dwayne's own family members, Afa and Sika, who were known as the Wild Samoans.

Maybe one wrestler will bring a chair crashing down on the head of another wrestler. It's all planned ahead of time by the wrestlers. But the fans watching the match do not know who the winner will be. This is what makes wrestling "an entertaining sport."

Rocky thought Dwayne would grow out of wanting to be a wrestler. But Rocky was wrong. Dwayne never did.

Peter Maivia, the Rock's grandfather, was a legend in the wrestling business. He weighed in at 320 pounds, and in the ring he was considered a fierce wrestler. Dwayne remembers him as being sweet, gentle, and kind with his family members.

A Hurricane

When Dwayne was eight years old, his family moved to Hawaii. It was there that he got to know his grandfather, Peter Maivia. Peter was big, tough, and honest, and Dwayne has great memories of the days he spent with him. In fact, Peter Maivia is one of the reasons Dwayne still considers Hawaii his home. "It represents so much of my heritage and my past and all that's important to me," he said.

When Dwayne was a teenager, his family moved from Hawaii to Bethlehem, Pennsylvania. Dwayne started tenth grade at Freedom High School.

The wrestling coach at his new school knew that Dwayne was a wrestling champion. The coach invited him to try out for the school's wrestling team. High school wrestling is an **amateur** sport. It isn't the same as professional wrestling. Dwayne was not allowed to use any of the moves he had learned from his father in the ring. Dwayne thought amateur wrestling was too easy and too boring. He left after one day of practice.

"Compared to the shows I had been raised on, it just wasn't much fun," he said.

Dwayne was an angry young man with a bad temper. His anger led him to make wrong choices. His temper got him into fights, and in 1987—just a few months after he arrived at Freedom High—he was suspended from school.

Dwayne knew he had to change his ways. The following year, when he was a junior in high school, he joined the football team and was made a team captain. Football helped Dwayne by giving him an outlet for his anger. It taught him that thinking things through and working hard instead of getting angry are good ways to take on a challenge and overcome it.

In his senior year of high school, Dwayne was named the eighth best high school football

Dwayne played a defensive position for the University of Miami Hurricanes. He wore the number 94.

player in the state of Pennsylvania. Many colleges offered him **scholarships** to play on their football teams. Dwayne signed on with the University of Miami in Florida to play with the Hurricanes. Unfortunately, he injured his shoulder during practice before the season began. He sat out most of his first season.

Dwayne's bad luck upset him. He no longer cared about doing well in college. He stopped going to his classes and began failing his courses. The coach gave him a warning. If he didn't bring up his grades, he would be off the team.

Dwayne got his life back on track. A woman named Dany Garcia helped. She was studying **finance** at the University of Miami. Before long, she and Dwayne were dating.

As Dwayne's shoulder injury improved, he was able to play more games. He played nine games as a freshman. On January 1, 1992, the Hurricanes beat the University of Nebraska Cornhuskers in the Orange Bowl. The Orange Bowl is an important college football game played in the Miami area each year.

National Football League (NFL) scouts study the college players during their regular seasons. The scouts look for players who will make good players for NFL teams. Dwayne was hoping to be **drafted** by the NFL.

On January 1, 1992, Dwayne helped lead the Miami Hurricanes to victory over the University of Nebraska Cornhuskers at the Orange Bowl.

Then bad fortune struck again. Dwayne hurt his back. He did not play well in his final season with the Hurricanes. He was not drafted by the NFL.

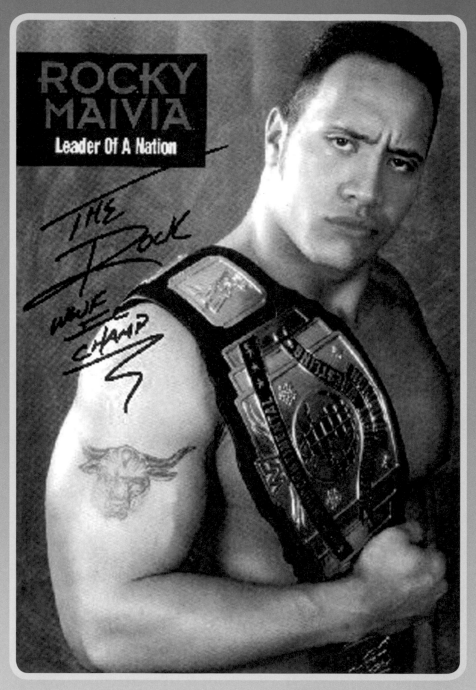

ROCKY MAIVIA
Leader Of A Nation

THE ROCK
WWF CHAMP

When he was young, Dwayne would put on his father's championship belts and pretend to be a champion wrestler. In 1998, Dwayne became the youngest World Champion in WWF history and received a championship belt of his own.

The People's Champion

Dwayne needed a new plan. The Calgary Stampeders, a team that is part of the Canadian Football League, asked him to be on its practice team. Dwayne said good-bye to Dany and his parents and moved to Canada.

When he got there, his life went from bad to worse. As a member of the practice team, he earned a very small salary. Often he didn't have enough money to buy food. He lived for days at a time on the sandwiches served at team meetings.

About a year after he moved to Canada, Dwayne realized his career as a football player was over. It was time to come home and join the "family business." It was time to become a pro wrestler. "[A] chapter in my life was ending and I wanted to turn the page and start a new one," he said.

Dwayne's parents were now living in Florida. He moved in with them and started training with his father.

Dwayne joined the WWF in 1996. Professional wrestlers have their own wrestling personalities. Some wrestlers are known by the outfits they wear when they wrestle. Almost all wrestlers have a special wrestling name. Rocky Johnson called himself Soulman. Dwayne took the name Rocky Maivia out of respect for both his father and his grandfather.

Dwayne's first big wrestling **competition** took place in New York City on November 16, 1996. It was called the Survivor Series. Millions of fans watched on pay-per-view television as eight wrestlers working in teams fought until there was one winner. That winner was Dwayne.

More wins followed. In 1997, Dwayne won WWF's **Intercontinental** (IN-ter-kon-tih-

NEN-tal) Championship. In 1998 he again won the Survivor Series. This win made him a WWF World Champion. At the time, he was the youngest World Champion in WWF history.

Around this time Dwayne changed his wrestling name to The Rock. His wrestling fans started calling him The People's Champion.

There was something else to celebrate in 1997. Dwayne and Dany were married on May 3 of that year.

People the world over love and admire Dwayne. He is especially loved in Samoa, the land of his mother's people. Dwayne visited Samoa in 2004 and met with the king, whose name was Malietoa Tanumafili II. The king crowned Dwayne a high chief. It is an honor that connects Dwayne to the Samoan royal family, and, Dwayne says, it "was a life-changing moment for me."

Madison Pettis and Dwayne Johnson attend the premiere of *The Game Plan*. Madison plays Dwayne's seven-year-old daughter, Peyton, in the movie.

No Longer "The Rock"

Dwayne won the WWF World Champion title seven times, more than any other professional wrestler. But by 2006 he wasn't doing a lot of wrestling.

That year, he made an announcement. "I am no longer a wrestler. . . . I am not 'The Rock.' I am Dwayne Johnson," he told a reporter.

Whether he is in the ring or out, Dwayne is still a winner.

In 2007 he starred in a Disney movie called *The Game Plan*. The movie earned almost $23 million its first weekend in theaters. He began working on a movie for 2009 called *The Tooth Fairy*. Once again Dwayne would be the

Dwayne Johnson's Rock Foundation helps young people from babies to twenty-two-year olds. Although he is a busy man, Dwayne takes time to visit the children helped by his foundation.

movie's star—playing the Tooth Fairy! Other films on his schedule were *Get Smart, Planet 51,* and *Race to Witch Mountain.*

Dwayne and Dany have one daughter, named Simone Alexandra. She was born on August 14, 2001. Dwayne and Dany love children. In 2006, they founded the Dwayne Johnson Rock Foundation. It is an organization that wants "to make every child smile." One way it does this is by helping children get physically fit. The foundation also donates toys to children's hospitals.

Dwayne and Dany's marriage ended in 2007. Although they are no longer married, they remain friends and continue to work together on the Rock Foundation. They also work together to raise Simone.

So far Dwayne Johnson has been a football player, a wrestler, and a movie star. What's next for the man who once called himself The Rock? Only time will tell—but one thing is sure. Whatever new adventure Dwayne Johnson finds himself involved in will be solid.

Rock solid.

Dwayne "The Rock" Johnson & Dany Garcia Johnson

October 2 20 *07*

PAY TO THE ORDER OF ___ **UƧTHLETICS** ___ $ 1,000,000.00

One Million Dollars and ᶜᶜ/₁ₒₒ ___ **DOLLARS**

MEMO Football Facilities Renovation Fund

27

CHRONOLOGY

1972 Dwayne Douglass Johnson is born on May 2 in Hayward, California.

1987 He attends Freedom High School in Bethlehem, Pennsylvania.

1989 He signs on to play football for the University of Miami.

1995 He graduates from the University of Miami with a degree in criminal justice.

1996 He makes his first pro wrestling appearance in the WWF *Survivor Series*.

1997 Dwayne marries Dany Garcia on May 3.

1998 He wins *Survivor Series* and becomes champion of the World Wresting Federation—his first championship title.

2001 He appears as Mathayus in the movie *The Mummy Returns*. His daughter, Simone Alexandra, is born on August 14.

2002 He appears as Mathayus in the movie *The Scorpion King*.

2004 He competes for the last time in *WrestleMania XX*; he visits Samoa and is named a high chief.

2006 He tells his fans he no longer wants to be called "The Rock."

2007 Dwayne stars in *The Game Plan*. He announces he and Dany will be getting a divorce.

2008 His foundation, the Rock Foundation, sponsors "Project Knapsack," a program that sends school supplies to children in Africa. He continues to make movies, including *Get Smart* and *Tooth Fairy*.

FILMOGRAPHY

2008 *Tooth Fairy*
      Planet 51
      Get Smart
2007 *The Game Plan*
2006 *Gridiron Gang*
      Southland Tales

2005 *Doom*
      Be Cool
2004 *Walking Tall*
2003 *The Rundown*
2002 *The Scorpion King*
2001 *The Mummy Returns*

FIND OUT MORE

Books

Burgan, Michael. *The Rock: Pro Wrestler Rocky Maivia*. Mankato, Minnesota: Capstone Press, 2002.

Gorman, Jacqueline Laks. *Dwayne "The Rock" Johnson*. Pleasantville, New York: Gareth Stevens, 2008.

Preller, James. *Rock Solid*. New York: Scholastic, 2000.

Ross, Dan. *The Story of the Wrestler They Call "The Rock."* Philadelphia: Chelsea House, 2001.

Works Consulted

Anderson, Jeffrey M. "Interview with Dwayne 'The Rock' Johnson." *San Francisco Examiner*, September 7, 2006. www.combustiblecelluloid.com/interviews/rockjohnson.shtml (accessed December 28, 2007).

"An Interview with the Rock." IGN. http://movies.ign.com/articles/357/357345pl.html.

Dodd, Johnny. "The Rock." *People.com*. August 26, 2004, http://www.people.com/people/article/0,,687063,00.html (Accessed March 11, 2008).

Dubin, Danielle, et. al. "Rock Solid." *People*, September 25, 2006. Vol. 66. No 13.

Fischer, Paul. "Rock On." *Tribute*, September 2003. Vol. 20 Issue 6.

Johnson, Dwayne, with Joe Layden. *The Rock Says* . . . New York: Avon, 2000.

Jordan, Julie. "Dwayne 'The Rock' Johnson & Wife Split Up." *People*, June 1, 2007.

Lopez, Molly. "The Rock's Sad Split." *People*, June 18, 2007, Vol. 67, Issue 24.

Paiva, Derek. "Multi-ethnic Wrestler Turned Movie Star Proud of Heritage." *Honolulu Advertiser*, Island Life Section, October 1, 2002.

"The Rock, the Kid and the King on the Screen." *USA Today*, September 27, 2007.

Sperling, Nicole. "Rock Steady." *Entertainment Weekly*, October 12, 2007.

"Wrestling Legend The Rock Tackles Hollywood in *The Mummy Returns*." *Jet*, May 21, 2001. Volume 99, Issue 23, p. 58.

"WWE Alumni: The Rock." WWE Superstars Website. http://www.wwe.com/superstars/wwealumni/therock/bio/ (Accessed January 18, 2008)

On the Internet

Dwayne Johnson Fansite
http://www.dwaynejohnsonfever.net/

The Rock Foundation
www.djrockfoundation.org/

Dwayne "The Rock" Biography
http://movies.go.com/dwayne-johnson/b737668

PHOTO CREDITS: Cover, p. I, 3— Guy Kinziger/WireImage; p. 4—Keith Hamshere/Universal Studios via Getty Images; p. 6—Kevin Winter/Getty Images; p. 8—Jonathan Scott; p. I7—Jed Jacobsohn/Getty Images; p. I9—Miami/Collegiate Images/Getty Images; p. 24— Jon Furniss/WireImage/Getty Images

GLOSSARY

amateur (AA-muh-chur)—Something done as a hobby or for fun.

ancient (AYN-chent)—Very old.

autobiography (aw-toh-by-AH-gruh-fee)—The story of a person's life, written by the person.

competition (kom-pih-TIH-shun)—A game in which two or more people play to win.

draft—To select for some purpose, such as to be on a team or to be in the military.

finance (FY-nants)—Having to do with money.

intercontinental (IN-ter-kon-tih-NEN-tal)—Involving teams from countries around the world.

scholarship (SKAH-lur-ship)—Money awarded to go to college.

INDEX